SCIENCE EXPLORERS

EARTH AND SPACE

Clare Hibbert

Enslow Publishing
101 W. 23rd Street
Suite 240
New York, NY 10011
USA
enslow.com

Published in 2019 by Enslow Publishing, LLC.
101 W. 23rd Street, Suite 240, New York, NY 10011

Cataloging-in-Publication Data

Names: Hibbert, Clare.
Title: Earth and space / Clare Hibbert.
Description: New York : Enslow Publishing, 2019. | Series: Science explorers | Includes glossary and index.
Identifiers: ISBN 9781978506695 (pbk.) | ISBN 9781978506428 (library bound) | ISBN 9781978506756 (6pack) | ISBN 9781978506497 (ebook)
Subjects: LCSH: Earth (Planet)—Juvenile literature. | Solar system—Juvenile literature. | Outer space—Juvenile literature.
Classification: LCC QB631.4 H625 2019 | DDC 525—dc23

Printed in the United States of America

To Our Readers: We have done our best to make sure all website addresses in this book were active and appropriate when we went to press. However, the author and the publisher have no control over and assume no liability for the material available on those websites or on any websites they may link to. Any comments or suggestions can be sent by email to customerservice@enslow.com.

Photo Credits:
Every attempt has been made to clear copyright. Should there be any inadvertent omission, please apply to the publisher for rectification.
Key: b-bottom, t-top, c-center, l-left, r-right
Alamy: 14–15 & 26br (Greg Vaughn), 15cr (Xinhua); ESO.org: cover bl & 19tr; Library of Congress: 18cl (SOHO/ESA), 20c, 22br (ESA/Hubble Heritage Team), 24c & 27bl (WMAP Science Team), 25bl, 32br; Pikaia Imaging: 20–21 & 27cl; Science Photo Library: 4–5 (Photo Insolite Realite), 8cr (Planetary Visions Ltd), 9br & 26tl (Spencer Sutton), 11cr (Carlos Clarivan), 12cr & 26bl (Gary Hincks), 14cr (Henning Dalhoff), 17b & 27tl (Mark Garlick), 18–19 (NASA/JPL), 22–23 & 27br (Chris Butler), 24br (Carlos Clarivan); Shutterstock: cover main (NASA), cover tl (Triff), cover br & 6tr (Diego Barucco), cover cl & 10c (sumikophoto), 4tr (adriaticfoto), 4c (Neal Pritchard Media), 4br (YC_Chee), 5tr (adike), 5br (NASA Images), 6–7 & 26tr (Vadim Sadovski/NASA), 6cr (Marc Ward/NASA), 8–9 (Therato), 8bl (Palau), 10–11 (Harvepino), 10bl (NoPainNoGain), 12–13 (Jakub Cejpek), 12bl & 30br (M Scheja), 14bl (robin2), 16–17 (godrick, vovan/NASA), 16cl (Castleski/NASA), 16bl (Monkey_Fish), 20tr (Designua), 20bl (Maria Zvonkova), 20cl (vectortatu), 24–25 (Andrea Danti), 26 cr (Chao pavit), 27tr (Jurik Peter), 28br (NokkieVector), 29cr (Oyls), 29bl (dani3315); Wikimedia Commons: 6bl (Davorka Herak and Marijan Herak), 13bl (Scottish National Gallery/Henry Raeburn), 18bl & 31br (Adler Planetarium and Astronomy Museum, Chicago/Brahe's Astronomiae instauratae), 23bl (Harvard University Library).

CONTENTS

Introduction

Science is amazing! It shapes our understanding of the universe and has transformed our everyday lives. At its heart, science is a way of collecting facts, developing ideas to explain those facts, and making predictions we can test.

Laboratory Learning

Chemistry investigates materials, from solids, liquids, and gases to the tiny atoms that make up everything. By understanding the rules behind how different kinds of matter behave, we can create new chemicals and materials with amazing properties.

Scientists can observe chemical reactions under a microscope.

Secrets of the Universe

Physics is the scientific study of energy, forces, mechanics, and waves. Energy includes heat, light, and electricity. Physics also looks at the structure of atoms and the workings of the universe. Even the galaxies obey the laws of physics!

Many forms of energy are involved in a storm.

Chimpanzees are one of around 7.8 million species of living animals.

Life on Earth

Natural history is the study of living things—the countless plants, animals, and other creatures that inhabit Earth now or which existed in the past. It studies how these organisms are influenced by each other and their environment. It also looks at the complex process of evolution—gradual change from one generation to the next.

How Organisms Work

Every living thing on Earth is made from cells—individual units that can combine and work together to create incredibly complex systems, including human beings. Biology involves the study of cells and the many tissues and organs that go into creating living things.

Electron microscopes let biologists study creatures such as this headlouse in extraordinary detail. The microscope itself is the result of a scientific breakthrough in the study of subatomic particles.

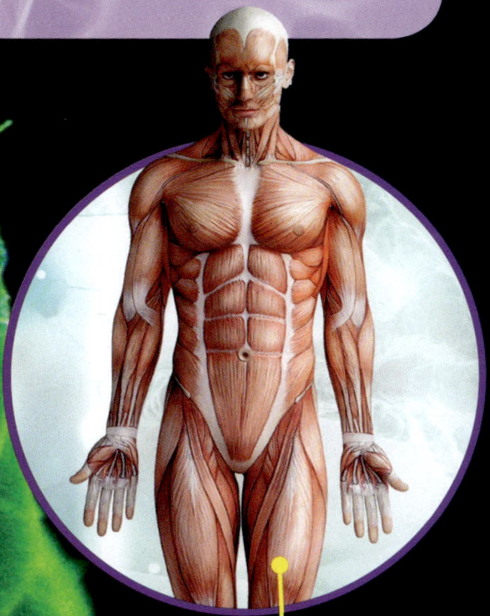

Biologists look at the workings of the human body.

Earth and Space Sciences

Geology is the study of our planet, Earth—how it was made, what it is made of, and how it has changed over time. Astronomy, meanwhile, looks at our place in the universe. It examines how Earth, the solar system, and other objects in space behave—as well as how the cosmos began, and how it might end.

Our planet, Earth.

Inside the Earth

Our planet is a huge ball of rock, 7,918 miles (12,742 km) across. It might seem solid all the way through, but not far beneath the surface is a deep layer called the mantle, which is a mix of semi-molten and solid rock. Deeper still, Earth's core is a swirling ball of molten and solid metal.

Earth was born about 4.6 billion years ago out of material left over from making the Sun. At first, even the surface was hot, molten rock. Our planet has been slowly cooling down ever since.

Layers within Layers

Earth's crust floats on the upper, semi-molten part of the mantle, and is cracked into giant plates. Rocks churn and grind past each other in the mantle, carrying heat from the core to the surface. The superhot core is made of iron and nickel, and mostly molten but solid at its heart.

Earth's Magnetic Field

The liquid part of Earth's metal core produces huge electric currents as it swirls, and these create a magnetic field. It is as if our planet is a giant magnet, with magnetic north and south poles close to the axis of its spin. This magnetic field forms a bubble around the Earth, which we call the magnetosphere.

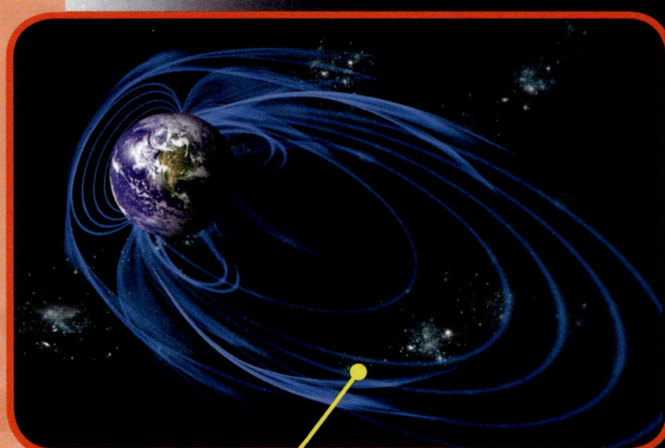

The magnetosphere repels dangerous particles from the Sun. Harmless, lower-energy solar particles fall into the atmosphere over the magnetic poles to create aurorae (see page 9).

AMAZING DISCOVERY

Scientist: Andrija Mohorovicic
Discovery: Earth's internal layers
Date: 1909
The story: Scientist Mohorovicic observed that earthquake shockwaves change their speed depending on their depth below the surface. He realized this was because they passed through different rock types and temperatures.

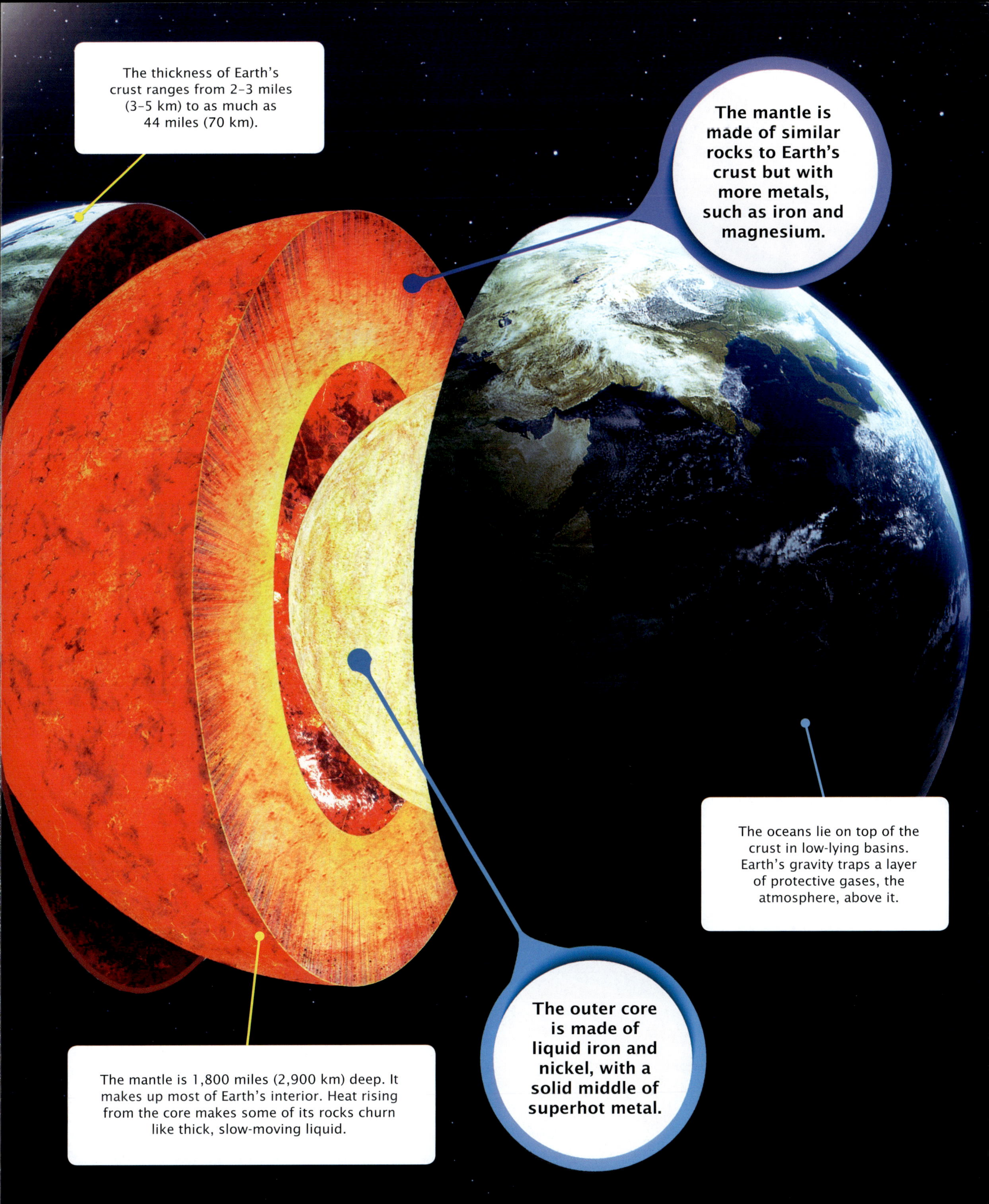
The thickness of Earth's crust ranges from 2–3 miles (3–5 km) to as much as 44 miles (70 km).
The mantle is made of similar rocks to Earth's crust but with more metals, such as iron and magnesium.
The oceans lie on top of the crust in low-lying basins. Earth's gravity traps a layer of protective gases, the atmosphere, above it.
The mantle is 1,800 miles (2,900 km) deep. It makes up most of Earth's interior. Heat rising from the core makes some of its rocks churn like thick, slow-moving liquid.
The outer core is made of liquid iron and nickel, with a solid middle of superhot metal.

Atmosphere and Weather

Space particles collide with atoms of gases in the atmosphere, give them energy, and make them glow.

Earth is surrounded by a thin but vital layer of gas called the atmosphere. It provides the air we breathe, creates a protective blanket that keeps out the worst extremes of hot and cold, and gives us a complex system of ever-changing weather.

Atmospheric Gases

Without an atmosphere absorbing and trapping the Sun's heat, our planet would be unbearably hot in the day and icy-cold at night. The main gases in the atmosphere are nitrogen and oxygen. Oceans, rocks, and living things absorb and produce different gases, creating a delicate balance.

Weather happens in the troposphere, the layer of the atmosphere that is closest to the Earth.

1. Warm air rises near the equator, cools, and sinks down closer to poles.

2. Winds are driven by the Earth's rotation, and by rising and falling air.

AMAZING DISCOVERY

Scientist: George Hadley
Discovery: Atmospheric circulation and winds
Date: 1735
The story: Amateur meteorologist (weather scientist) Hadley was the first person to realize that wind patterns were due to the Earth spinning on its axis and the way air rises in hot areas and sinks in colder ones.

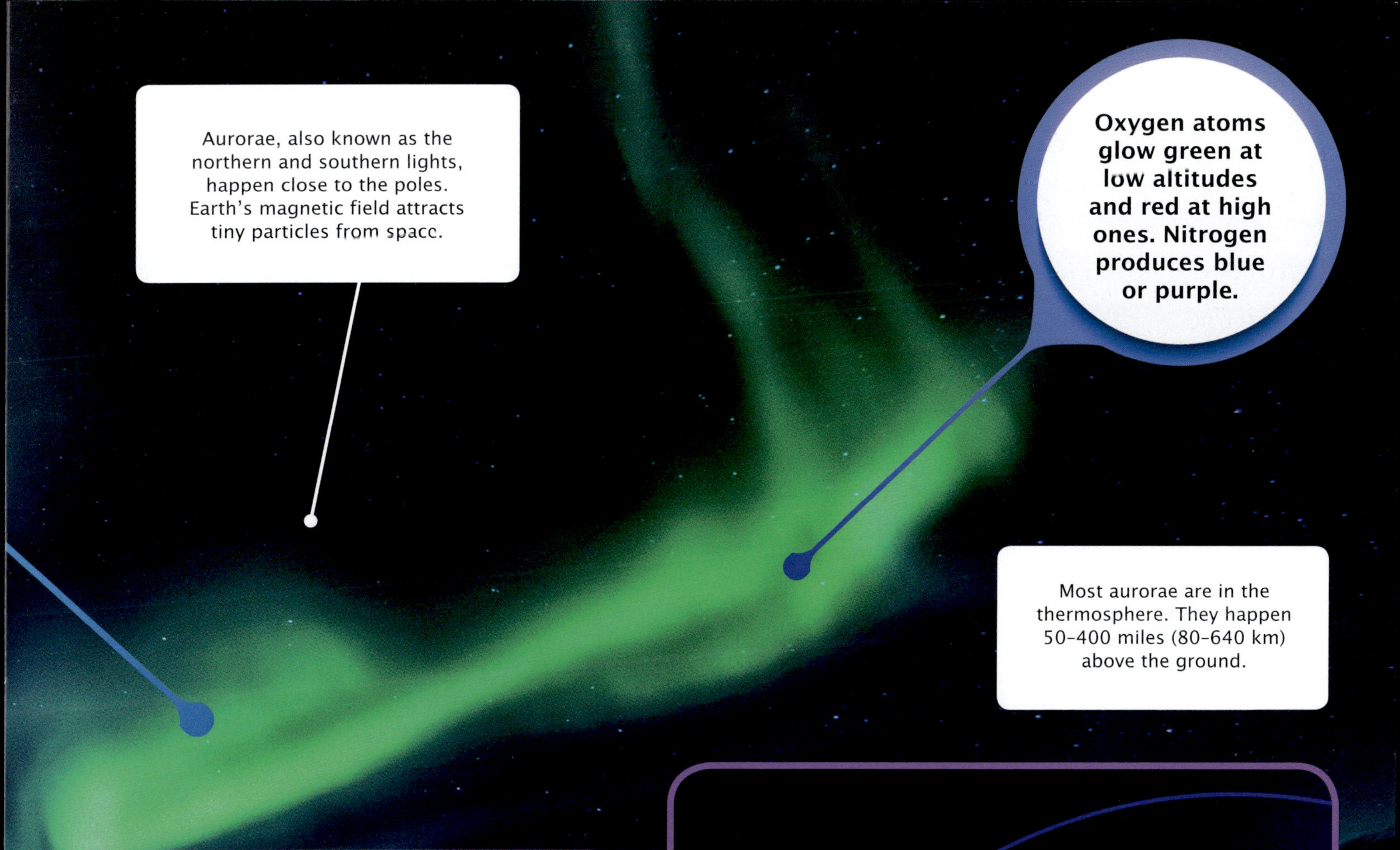

Balancing the Climate

Carbon dioxide (CO_2) is called a greenhouse gas because it traps heat like the glass of a greenhouse. The CO_2 in our atmosphere keeps our planet warm. However, burning fossil fuels such as coal and oil creates more CO_2 than there used to be. This is heating the planet at a faster rate and changing our climate.

The atmosphere is divided into layers that stretch out into space. It gets thinner the higher we go.

1. TROPOSPHERE up to 7.5 miles (12 km)
2. STRATOSPHERE 7.5–31 miles (12–50 km)
3. MESOSPHERE 31–50 miles (50–80 km)
4. THERMOSPHERE 50–435 miles (80-700 km)
5. EXOSPHERE 435–6,214 miles (700–10,000 km)

Earth's Water

Earth is the only planet in our solar system with the right surface temperature for water to exist as liquid, solid ice, and gas (water vapor). The water cycle changes water between these forms, moves it around, and shapes our planet.

Erosion

Water is an irresistible force. Rivers and slow-moving bodies of ice called glaciers wear away and erode Earth's rocks. Seas beat at cliffs. Over thousands of years, water shapes the landscape and transports ground-down particles, or sediment, into low-lying areas. Water is an even more powerful erosive force than wind or extreme heat or cold.

Water naturally flows downhill. Rainfall over land finds its way to the oceans through rivers, lakes, and streams.

The Grand Canyon in Arizona is an 1.1 mile- (1,800 m) deep valley. It has been carved out by the winding Colorado River over the past six million years or more.

AMAZING DISCOVERY

Scientist: Benjamin Franklin
Discovery: The Gulf Stream
Date: 1769–1770
The story: The Gulf Stream current of warm, fast-moving water flowing north and east across the Atlantic was known to earlier sailors, but Franklin was first to study it in detail. He saw it was part of a bigger pattern of ocean movements.

Where winter snowfall does not completely melt in summer, it builds up into creeping layers of ice called glaciers.

Up to four percent of Earth's atmosphere is water vapor. When vapor condenses to form clouds in the air, droplets can fall to the ground as rain or snow.

Water Distribution

Most water is mixed with salty minerals in Earth's seas. Fresh water makes up just 3.5 percent, and most of it is frozen into ice around the poles and on high mountains. Liquid fresh water is found in lakes, rivers, and underground. There is also a small but vital amount of water vapor in the atmosphere.

Heat from the Sun drives ocean water into the air as moisture. It returns to the ground as rain and snow, creating rivers and lakes and shaping the landscape as it flows back to the sea.

Ice caps like the ones over Greenland and Antarctica trap frozen water on top of land.

Earth's Crust

Earth's crust is part of what makes our planet unique. It is broken into seven major plates (and many smaller ones) that move around on top of the slowly churning mantle. Over millions of years these plates rearrange Earth's continents and oceans in a process that is called plate tectonics.

Floating Continents

The crust floats on top of the mantle because it is made of lighter rocks. Where the crust is highest (on continents or at high mountain ranges), it also stretches down the deepest—rather like an iceberg. Continental crust can be up to 44 miles (70 km) thick.

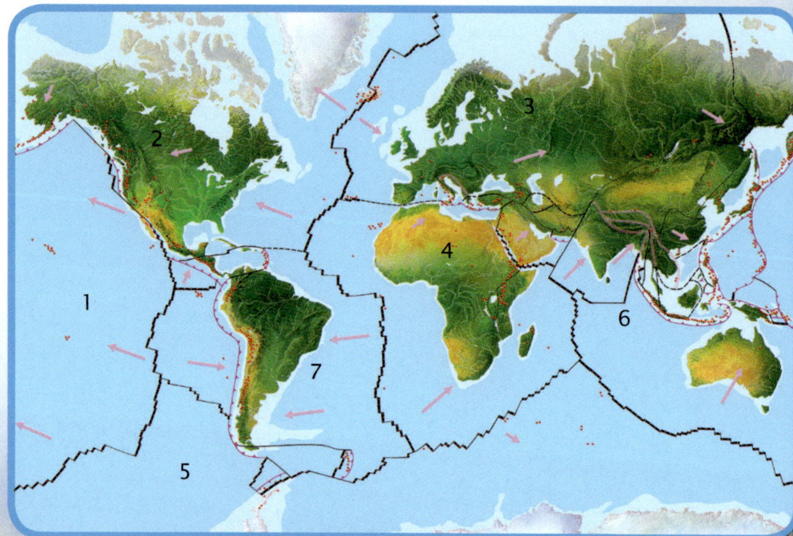

MAJOR TECTONIC PLATES
1. PACIFIC PLATE 2. NORTH AMERICAN PLATE
3. EURASIAN PLATE 4. AFRICAN PLATE 5. ANTARCTIC PLATE
6. INDO-AUSTRALIAN PLATE (broken into Australian and Indian plates)
7. SOUTH AMERICAN PLATE

Places such as China's Striped Mountains show how sedimentary rock forms in strata, or layers.

Three Types of Rock

Igneous rocks, such as basalt, form from cooled magma, either underground or where it's erupted as lava from a volcano. Sedimentary rocks, such as sandstone, are made when ground-down particles of rock settle and compress. Metamorphic rocks are created when another kind of rock is put under great heat or pressure, changing the minerals it contains—heated limestone becomes marble, for example.

Some mountains are made from igneous rocks that solidified from molten lava.

Even the highest mountains are steadily worn away over time by heat, cold, wind, and rain.

Some mountains contain rocks that formed on the seabed millions of years ago.

AMAZING DISCOVERY

Scientist: James Hutton
Discovery: Cycles in Earth's history
Date: 1785
The story: Scottish geologist Hutton showed how the three main types of rock relate to each other because of repeated cycles of settling, lifting up, and wearing away, stretching back over hundreds of millions of years.

Volcanoes and Earthquakes

Powerful forces are unleashed in places where the plates of Earth's crust come together. Huge masses of rock crumple against or grind past each other and trigger devastating earthquakes. Where crust is driven down into the mantle, molten rock escapes through chains of volcanoes.

Violent eruptions happen when trapped gas bursts from pockets of magma beneath Earth's surface.

Plate Boundaries

If plates meet head-on, what happens next depends on the types of crust involved. Thin ocean crust will be pushed under thick continental crust, and as it melts in the mantle it will release heat that creates volcanoes. Where two continental plates meet, they buckle to create towering mountain ranges.

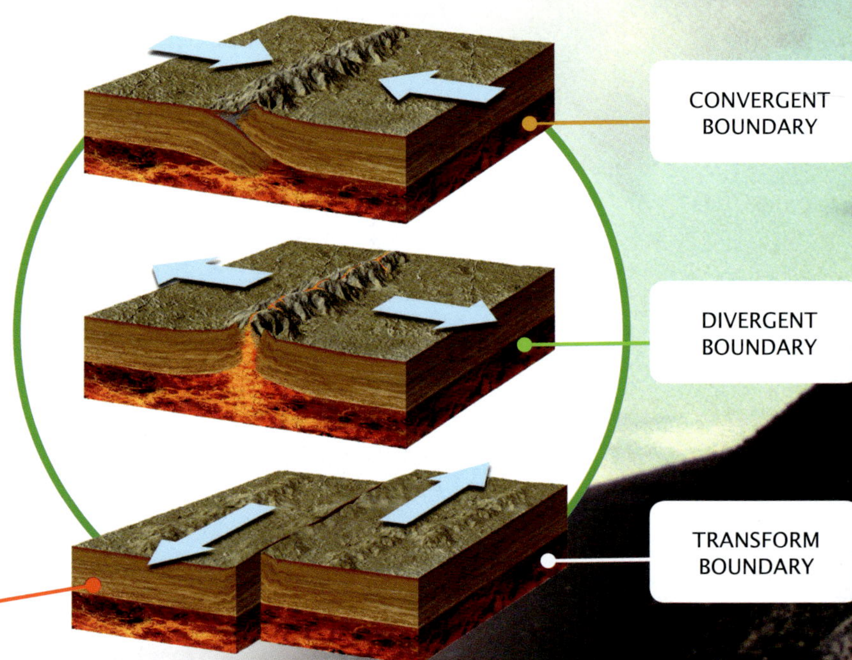

Plates collide at convergent boundaries, pull apart (often beneath the oceans) at divergent boundaries, and grind past each other at transform boundaries.

AMAZING DISCOVERY

Scientist: Alfred Wegener
Discovery: Tectonic drift
Date: 1912
The story: Meteorologist Wegener noticed how the edges of widely separated landmasses fit together like a jigsaw. He suggested that continents move slowly around on Earth's crust, but his idea only began to be accepted in the 1950s.

Volcanoes form where tectonic movements heat and melt underground rock to form molten magma. When magma erupts at the surface, it is called lava.

Earthquakes

When Earth's crust suddenly shifts, it triggers waves of disturbance called earthquakes. This can happen when tectonic plates collide or when they grind sideways past each other. The waves spread through the crust and also down through the Earth. Sometimes the vibrations can be detected on the other side of the world.

Many of our biggest cities, such as Mexico City, are built in earthquake zones. Unfortunately scientists cannot yet predict exactly where or when a disastrous quake will strike.

Volcanoes and earthquakes happen at plate boundaries, and also above random "hot spots" in Earth's mantle.

Liquid lava from volcanoes cools down rapidly. It solidifies into new igneous rocks.

Earth and Moon

Earth is not alone on its journey through space. A rocky satellite world we call the Moon orbits our planet every 27.3 days. At 2,160 miles (3,474 km) across, the Moon is a quarter of Earth's diameter. It is up to 248,548 miles (400,000 km) away—close enough to have a great influence on our planet.

A Lifeless World

The Moon's small size and gravity mean it cannot hold onto an atmosphere, and it has no life, surface water, or tectonic plates. Its main features are bright highlands and dark, smooth "seas" of solidified lava from ancient volcanoes. The highlands are covered in craters from when the Moon was bombarded by space rocks early in its history.

Volcanic activity ended on the Moon about three billion years ago. Since then, only a few new craters have appeared from asteroid impacts.

Dust thrown out during asteroid impacts forms bright streaks across the surface.

The Moon doesn't have its own light—it reflects the Sun's. As it orbits us, we see different amounts of the lit-up side and it seems to change shape. The different shapes are called the phases of the Moon.

AMAZING DISCOVERY

Scientists: The *Apollo* astronauts
Discovery: Origins of the Moon
Date: 1969–1972
The story: Rocks collected during the *Apollo* Moon landings showed scientists back on Earth how the Moon was made. It probably formed from molten rock ejected when a Mars-sized world collided with the young Earth 4.51 billion years ago.

The Moon has no air to protect it. Temperatures range from 260°F (127°C) in sunlight to -280°F (-173°C) in darkness.

Darker "seas" show where volcanic lava filled huge craters on the Moon's surface.

Time and Tide

The Moon's gravity pulls on the near side of Earth. This creates bulges in Earth's oceans directly beneath, and opposite, the Moon. As Earth rotates each day under these bulges, the seas rise and fall.

Tidal bulges can cancel each other out (1), resulting in weak tides.

The Sun's gravity creates its own tidal bulge. It can either work against the Moon's pull (1) or with it (2).

When tidal bulges join together (2), it results in especially strong tides.

Solar System

Earth is the third of eight planets orbiting our local star, the Sun. The part of space caught in the Sun's pull is called the solar system. As well as the planets, it contains countless smaller worlds—rocky asteroids in the inner solar system, and frozen comets and ice dwarfs farther out.

The Planets

Mercury, Venus, Earth, and Mars are closest to the Sun. Earth is the largest of these rocky planets. Farther out lie the giant planets—Jupiter (the biggest of all), Saturn, Uranus, and Neptune. Each of the giant planets has rings and a family of moons.

Saturn's bright ring system is made up of countless icy fragments in orbit around it.

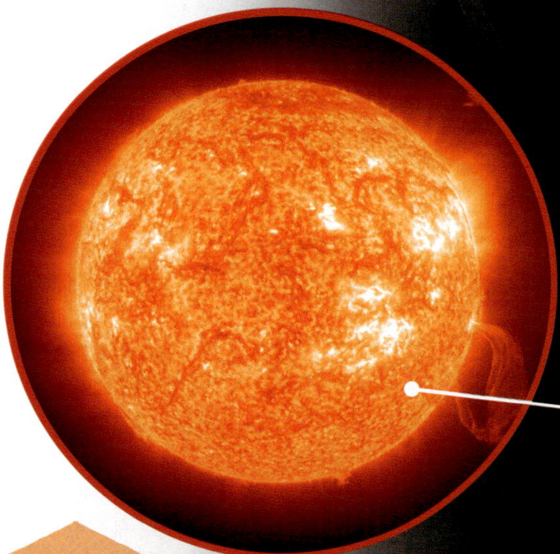

The Sun is a massive, fiery ball of gas, about 870,000 miles (1.4 million km) across. It contains 99.8 percent of the solar system's mass, and it provides heat and light to all of the planets.

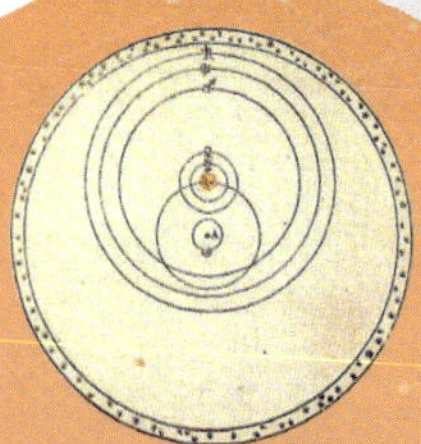

AMAZING DISCOVERY

Scientists: Tycho Brahe, Johannes Kepler
Discovery: Orbits of the planets
Date: 1572–1619
The story: Kepler used Brahe's careful observations of Mars to show that planets do not move in perfect circles. He explained that their paths are elliptical (stretched), and that they move faster when they are closer to the Sun.

Edge of the Solar System

Neptune's orbit takes it 30 times farther from the Sun than Earth, but this is not the edge of the solar system. Beyond this outermost planet lies the Kuiper Belt, a ring of small, icy worlds including Pluto. And beyond that is the Oort Cloud, a shell of icy comets that is 100,000 times Earth's distance from the Sun.

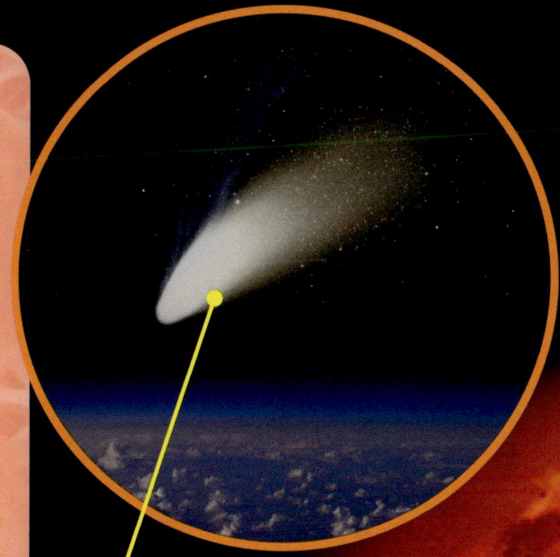

Icy comets are sometimes pushed into orbits that bring them close to the Sun. As they heat up, their ice turns to vapor and they can grow spectacular tails.

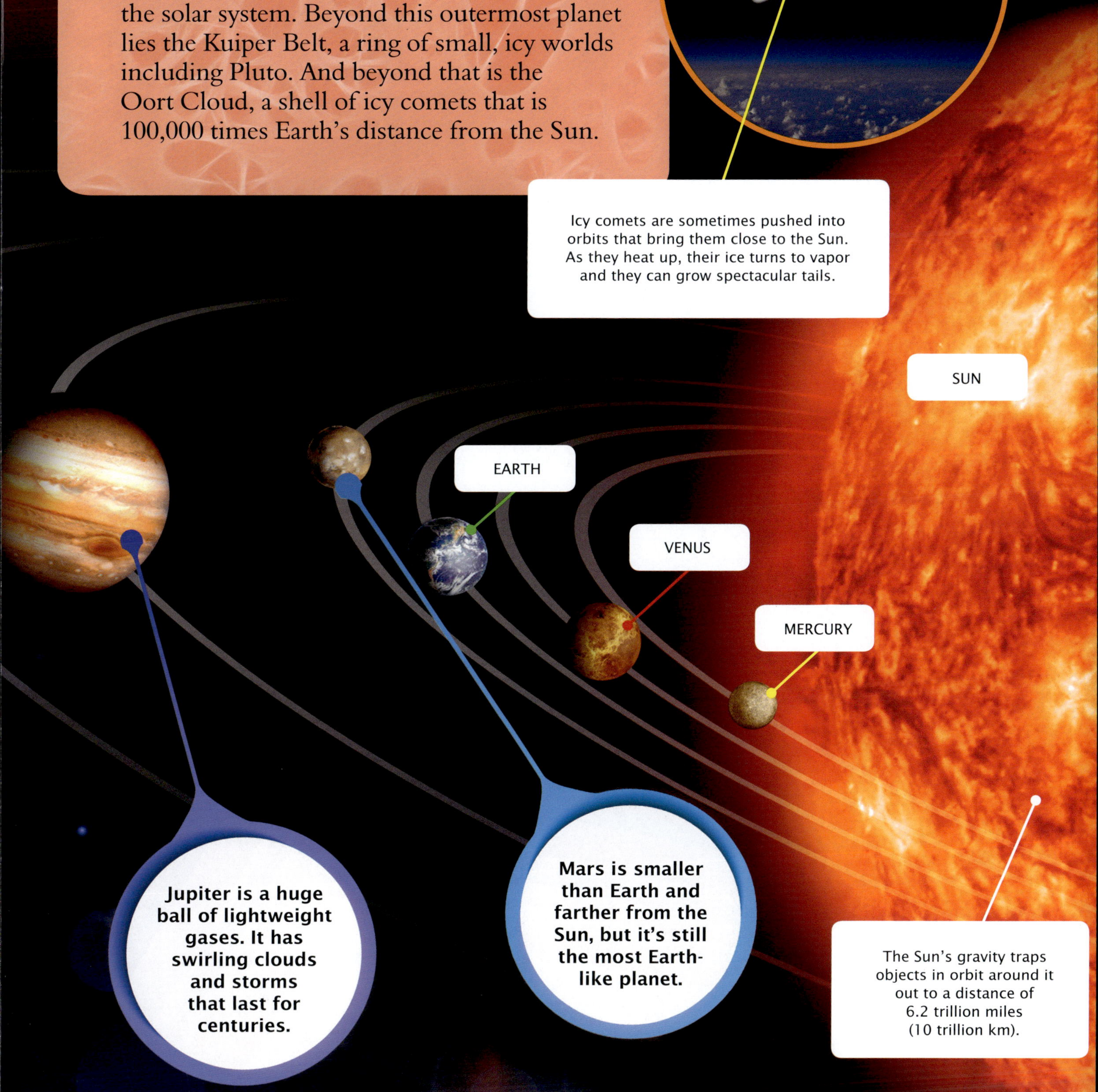

Jupiter is a huge ball of lightweight gases. It has swirling clouds and storms that last for centuries.

Mars is smaller than Earth and farther from the Sun, but it's still the most Earth-like planet.

The Sun's gravity traps objects in orbit around it out to a distance of 6.2 trillion miles (10 trillion km).

Stars and the Galaxy

Our Sun is just one of 200 billion stars in a vast, slowly spinning spiral galaxy called the Milky Way. The Sun is a very average star and only appears bright because it is nearby. Other stars are so far that their light takes many years to reach Earth.

Types of Stars

A star's brightness in the sky depends on its distance from Earth and how much light energy it's producing. Stars shine from nuclear fusion reactions that can last for billions of years. They vary from lower-energy dwarfs, 50,000 times fainter than the Sun, to giants 30 million times brighter.

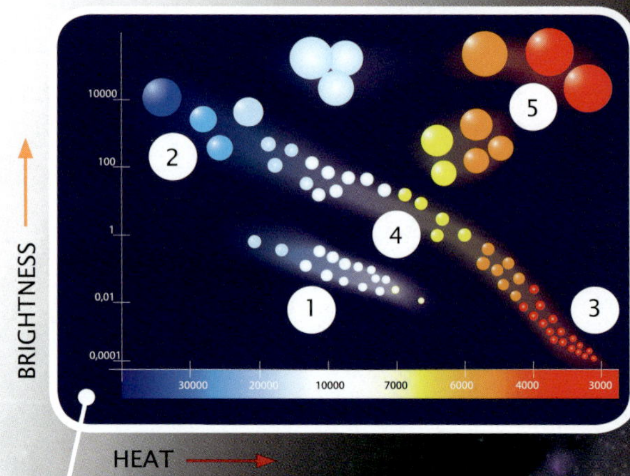

This graph shows the kinds of star at different temperatures and brightnesses. Red stars are cooler and blue ones are hotter.

KEY TO STAR TYPES

1. WHITE DWARFS
2. BLUE GIANTS
3. RED DWARFS
4. SUNLIKE STARS
5. RED SUPERGIANTS

How Stars Die

When a star runs out of nuclear fuel in its core, it goes through a series of changes as it dies. First it grows in size and brightens, becoming a red giant. All but the heaviest stars then puff off their outer layers, leaving behind a burned-out core called a white dwarf.

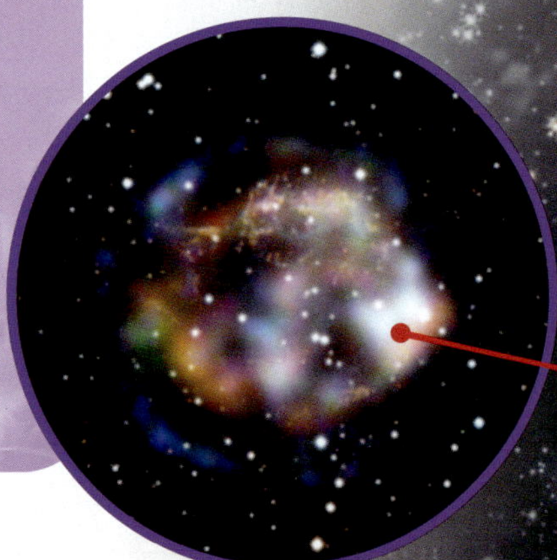

The most massive stars die in an explosion called a supernova that can briefly outshine an entire galaxy. All that's left of the star is an expanding bubble of superhot gas.

AMAZING DISCOVERY

Scientists: Ejnar Hertzsprung, Henry Norris Russell
Discovery: Types of stars
Date: 1910–1913
The story: Hertzsprung and Russell found that nearly all stars follow a simple rule—the brighter they are, the hotter they are. Only a few stars are bright but cool (red giants) or faint but hot (white dwarfs).

The Milky Way is about 120,000 light-years across. Our solar system orbits its core every 240 million years.
At the heart of the Milky Way, billions of red and yellow stars orbit a huge black hole.
Stars form from collapsing clouds of gas. They begin their lives in clusters of hot blue and white stars.
The Milky Way is a huge flattened disc of gas, dust, and stars. New stars are born in spiral regions that wind their way out from the galaxy's core.

The Universe

The universe is (probably) everything that exists—a vast and perhaps endless expanse of space and time. Our Milky Way is just one of more than 100 billion galaxies. Powerful telescopes let us see millions of these galaxies spread out across space.

Spiral galaxies appear blue and white because of the young, bright stars in their discs.

Measuring the Universe

Astronomers can work out how far away other galaxies are by looking for stars called variables. These stars change their brightness over time and some follow a repeating cycle. We can compare the variable's true brightness with how bright it appears to work out its distance—usually many millions of light-years. Another method is to look for exploding stars or supernovae in distant galaxies, and see how bright they get.

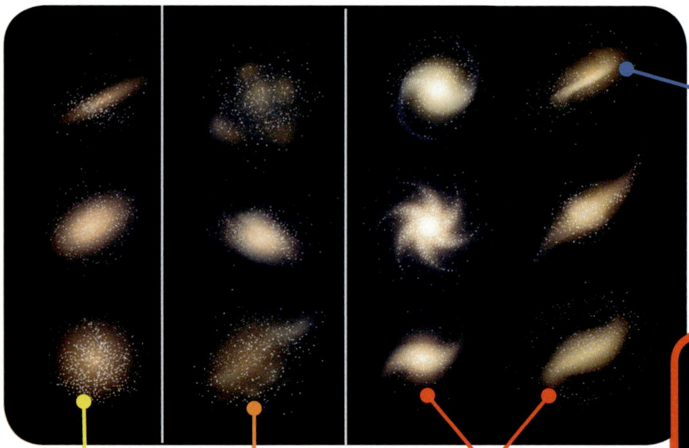

Galaxies have many shapes. Most of them are spirals like our Milky Way, ball-shaped ones called ellipticals, or shapeless clouds of gas called irregulars.

Cosmic Expansion

When astronomers first worked out the true distance to nearby galaxies, they noticed a pattern—the farther away a galaxy is, the faster it is moving away from us. This is because space itself is expanding, carrying galaxies away from each other like the raisins in a rising fruit cake.

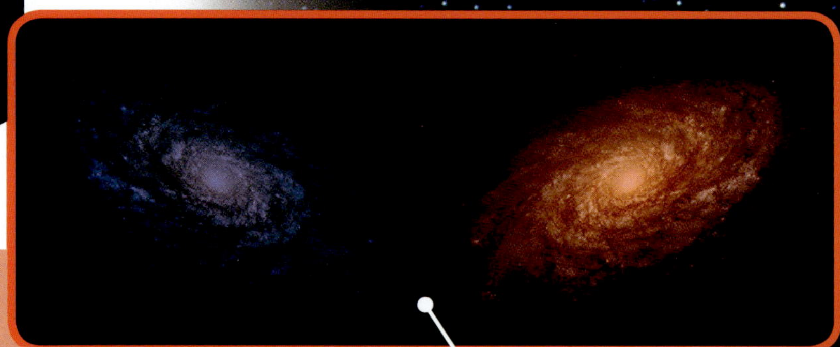

Astronomers discovered the motion of stars and galaxies by measuring the "red shift" in their light. An object moving away from Earth has its light stretched to longer, redder wavelengths, while one moving toward us appears "blue shifted."

AMAZING DISCOVERY

Scientists: Henrietta Swan Leavitt (left), Edwin Hubble
Discovery: The scale of the universe
Date: 1908–1929
The story: Leavitt was the first to spot the link between how some variable stars change over time and their true brightness. Hubble used this to estimate the distance of nearby galaxies, and to discover cosmic expansion.

The Big Bang and Beyond

The universe was born out of a huge explosion that took place about 13.8 billion years ago. This Big Bang released huge amounts of energy that made all the matter in the universe. It even created space and time themselves.

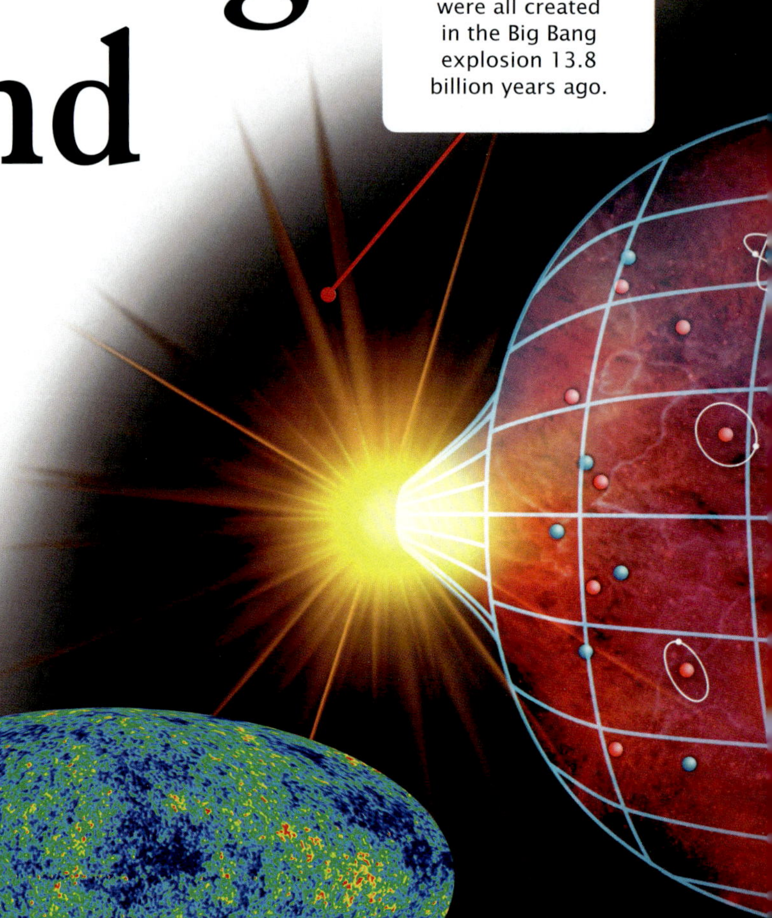

Matter, energy, space, and time were all created in the Big Bang explosion 13.8 billion years ago.

Evidence for the Big Bang

The discovery that all galaxies are moving apart shows that they must have been much closer together in the distant past, when the universe would have been much denser and hotter. We can even see the faint afterglow of the Big Bang—waves of cosmic microwave background radiation (CMBR).

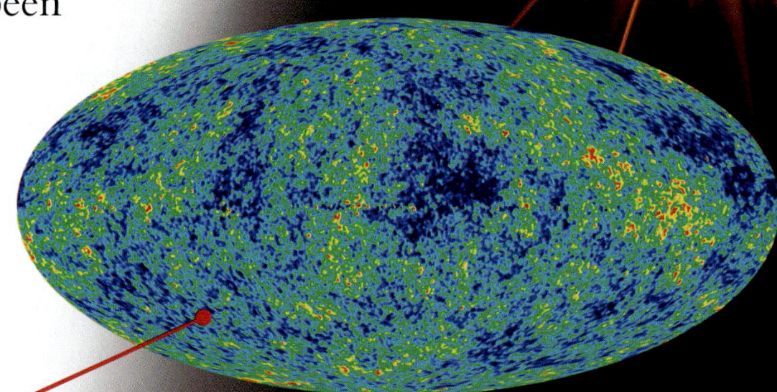

The CMBR is a faint glow of radio waves that comes from all over the sky. Brighter and darker areas show the seeds of galaxy clusters in the early universe.

Will the Universe Ever End?

The universe has three possible futures. Gravity from all the matter within it could slow its expansion and pull everything back to a Big Crunch. Another idea is that a mysterious force called dark energy could push everything apart in a Big Rip. Finally, space might just keep on expanding.

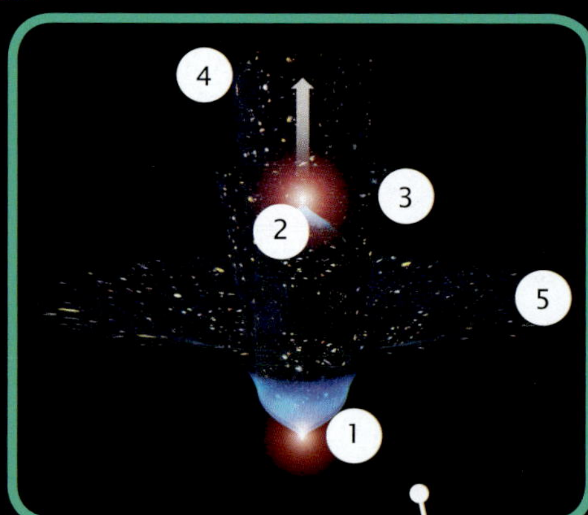

The universe began with the Big Bang (1). It may end in an explosive Big Crunch (2) or keep expanding (3). This illustration also shows what would happen if the universe had no dark energy (4) or if it had so much (5) that it would eventually tear itself apart in a Big Rip.

AMAZING DISCOVERY

Scientists: Arno Penzias, Robert Wilson
Discovery: Cosmic microwave background radiation (CMBR)
Date: 1964
The story: Astronomers had proposed that the Big Bang might have left faint radiation behind. Penzias and Wilson found it by accident when, testing a new radio antenna, they found a strange glow coming from all over the sky.

Fun Facts

Now that you have discovered lots about Earth and space, boost your knowledge further with these 10 quick facts!

Geologists estimate that the boundary between Earth's solid inner and liquid outer cores is 10,832°F (6,000°C)—hotter than the surface of the Sun.

At the outer edge of the exosphere, 6,214 miles (10,000 km) above Earth's surface, lightweight gas particles are constantly blown away into space.

If all of Earth's water was collected into a ball, it would be about 860.6 miles (1,385 km) across—just 0.1 percent of our planet's entire volume.

Most tectonic plates move around 1 in (2.5 cm) per year, but the South Pacific's Nazca Plate is racing along more than twice as fast.

The 1883 eruption of the Krakatoa volcano in Indonesia was the loudest sound in recorded history. People heard the explosion 3,100 miles (5,000 km) away!

Energy from Earth's tides makes the Moon move about 1.5 in (3.8 cm) farther away from us each year.

The asteroid belt between Mars and Jupiter contains about 1.5 million space rocks that are bigger than 0.6 miles (1 km) across.

Astronomers measure the distance to stars in light-years—how far light travels in a year. One light-year is 5.9 trillion miles (9.5 trillion km).

Looking across space is the same as looking back in time—the light we detect from the most distant galaxies has been on its way to us for 13.4 billion years.

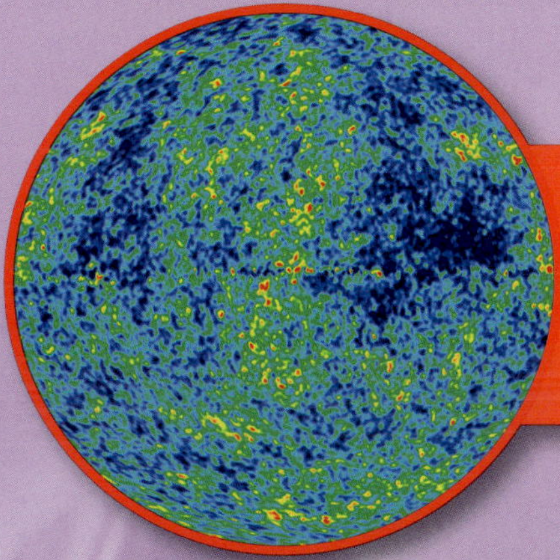

CMBR warms the entire universe to just 37°F (2.7°C) above the coldest possible temperature, –459.67°F (–273.15°C) or absolute zero.

Your Questions Answered

We know an incredible amount about our planet, the solar system, and the universe. But there is always more to discover. Scientists are still researching our Earth's history and the galaxies in our universe, and are continuing to find out more incredible details. Here are some questions about Earth and space that can help you understand more about this vast and fascinating topic.

Is it possible to predict volcanic eruptions?

Volcanologists (scientists who study volcanoes) are getting better and better at predicting volcanic eruptions. Active volcanoes are monitored for early signs of an eruption. In order of appearance, these are: 1. Series of small earthquakes, as the magma rises up through the Earth's crust; 2. Temperature rises around the volcano as the activity in the crust increases; 3. Release of gases, especially sulphur, shortly before the eruption. Once these signs have been identified, people who live close to the volcano are evacuated to safety.

What is the strongest earthquake recorded?

Since 1935, scientists around the world have used the Richter scale to measure the strength of an earthquake. Named after the American geologist Charles F. Richter, the scale classifies an earthquake of up to 3 as weak, 4–5 as medium, and anything over 6 as strong. The most powerful earthquake recorded was the Valdivia earthquake in Chile in 1960. It scored 9.5 on the Richter scale.

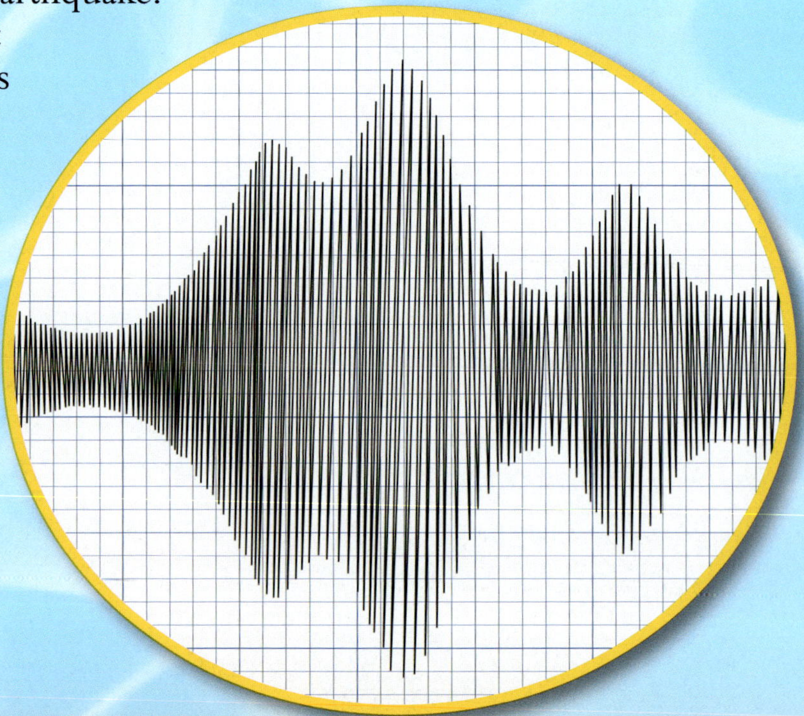

Scientists measure the vibrations in the Earth's crust to determine the strength of an earthquake.

Will time travel ever be possible?

There are a number of scientists who are studying the possibilities of time travel. They make two distinctions—journeying forward in time, and journeying back, into the past. If we had the technology available to us, it should be possible for someone to get on a spacecraft, accelerate continuously, travel to the middle of our galaxy, and then return to Earth, with time passing at a much slower rate for them than on Earth. For them 40 years would have passed, while on Earth, 60,000 years would have gone by. Scientists aren't entirely sure whether travel into the past is possible or not.

Do mountain ranges keep rising along convergent boundaries?

Mountains that exist due to tectonic plates crashing into each other will continue to rise as long as the tectonic plates carry on pushing into each other. There are other influences that influence the height of mountains, such as erosion and the effects of possible earthquakes. However, even given those effects, mountain ranges such as the Himalayas can grow by over 0.3 in (1 cm) per year.

In 2015, an earthquake in Nepal resulted in parts of the Himalayas dropping in height by about 23 in (60 cm).

Do we know when our Sun will die?

As with all other stars in the universe, our Sun will also eventually run out of energy and die. Scientists are agreed that this will happen in about five billion years. It will initially turn into a red giant, swelling to between 100 and 1,000 times its size, and then cool down to become a white dwarf.

At its largest, our Sun may swallow Mercury, Venus, and even Earth during its existence as a red giant.

Glossary

altitude The height of an object in relation to sea or ground level.

asteroid A small, rocky body orbiting the Sun.

atom The smallest possible particle of a chemical element.

black hole A region of space that has such an intense gravitational field, it doesn't even emit radiation.

comet A body that travels through space and is made of ice and dust. When approaching the Sun, the comet displays a "tail" of gas and dust.

condense To make something more dense.

galaxy A system of stars, held together by gravity.

glacier A slowly moving mass of ice.

gravity A force which tries to pull two objects together. Earth's gravity is what keeps us on the ground, and what makes objects fall.

lava Molten rock erupted from a volcano.

magma Molten rock beneath the Earth's crust.

magnetosphere The magnetic field surounding Earth (or another planet).

molten The liquid state of materials with a high melting point.

orbit To move around an object on a particular path, such as the Moon orbiting Earth.

satellite An object that is in orbit around Earth.

star Huge balls of gas in space that are held together by gravity. Their core is incredibly hot and they produce energy in the form of heat and light.

strata Layers of rock in the ground that form over millions of years.

water vapor Water in its gaseous form.

Further Information

BOOKS

DK Publishing. *Knowledge Encyclopedia: Space!* London, UK: DK Children's, 2015.

Ignotofsky, Rachel. *The Wondrous Workings Of Planet Earth: Understanding Our World And Its Ecosystems*. Danvers, MA: Ten Speed Press, 2018.

Lowe, Stuart and Chris North. *Cosmos: The Infographic Book Of Space.* London, UK: Aurum Press, 2017.

Mould, Steve. *How To Be A Scientist*. London, UK: DK Children, 2017.

Stowell, Louie. *The Usborne Official Astronaut's Handbook*. London, UK: Usborne Publishing, 2015.

WEBSITES

BBC Bitesize Space
https://www.bbc.com/education/topics/z8c9q6f
Explore this BBC webpage and find out much more about our solar system.

Geography for Kids
http://www.sciencekids.co.nz/geography.html
Visit this website to discover Earth activities, videos, quizzes, and much more!

What Is the International Space Station?
https://www.nasa.gov/audience/forstudents/5-8/features/nasa-knows/what-is-the-iss-58.html
Explore all there is to know about the International Space Station.

Index